MONEY MANAGEMENT

A Step By Step Guide For Beginners To Start Saving Money, Master Personal Financial Skills And Learn The Best Strategies To Reach Financial Freedom

WRITTEN BY
GRANT RAMSEY

Sommario

Introduction 6

Chapter 1: Where does your money go? 9

   How to eliminate unnecessary expenses 14

Chapter 2 Budgeting..16

   What is a budget 17

   Types of budgets 20

   Why is budgeting important 21

   How to stick to your budget............................22

Chapter 3: The easiest way to save......................24

   How to save on home expenses 26

Chapter 4: How To Get Out Of Debt 33

   Good debt and Bad debt 34

Chapter 5: Credit Cards 41

   Here are some credit card terms you should know 43

   Pros and cons of using a credit card 44

   Safeguarding your Credit 48

Chapter 6: Start Saving..50

   How to keep money 52

   How to start saving 54

Chapter 7: Increasing Your Income......................56

How to increase your income at work..............57

How to negotiate your income 59

Multiple sources of income..............................62

How to have a second source of income 64

Chapter 8: Investing Your Money 69

Warning: Approach with caution.....................70

Start investing small amounts of money 71

Step 1: separate your short-term and long-term goals...72

    Short-term investments 72

    Long-term investment...................................73

Step two: how much money do you want to invest 74

Step 3: allocate your assets a target.................75

Step 4: evaluate the fees and keep them as low as possible 75

Real estate investment for beginners..............76

Investing in stocks for beginners 77

Conclusion 78

© Copyright 2019 - All rights reserved.

The content contained within this book may not be reproduced, duplicated or transmitted without direct written permission from the author or the publisher.

Under no circumstances will any blame or legal responsibility be held against the publisher, or author, for any damages, reparation, or monetary loss due to the information contained within this book. Either directly or indirectly.

Legal Notice:

This book is copyright protected. This book is only for personal use. You cannot amend, distribute, sell, use, quote or paraphrase any part, or the content within this book, without the consent of the author or publisher.

Introduction

Money affects every aspect of our lives. We think about it, use it, earn it, and worry about it. But, do we sit to examine how money works? What makes it a significant part of our lives? How it affects us when we have it and when our accounts are running low?

Most probably not, but if you are looking to improve your financial situation, save more, invest more, and ultimately become financially free, you must examine your relationship with money. What most of us fail to admit is money has high value only because we have given it the value. Looking closely at what money is, we will discover that it is a medium of exchange and a way to store value.

We use it to trade when we agree to exchange it for something else (medium of exchange) and use it to hold value until later (store value). When we use it to as a medium of exchange, we can either keep the money in cash or in a bank account where we can easily access it for another transaction later.

In real sense, therefore, money has no inherent value. You can't eat money, use it as medicine or for anything useful. Materially, a one-hundred-dollar bill is the same as a twenty-dollar bill. Value is only based on an agreement, but the actual currency can be anything. You can either pay in cash or electronic and most recently, through blockchain technology.

Traditionally, barter trade was the medium of exchange. You give me hide skin so I am warm during winter and I provide you with the grain you can eat throughout the seasons. The matching needs determined the value. However, it was hard to store value and sometimes even hard for the universe to align, so you have matching needs with another person.

The use of money made all these challenges a thing of the past and increased the value of items. How much value you give determines how much money you earn. However, the value we attach to money can increase or decrease depending on how valuable we think it is. For instance, when money gets less value, we use more money to buy the same things, and if this continues, money becomes worthless. The opposite is true. The less we use to buy the same commodities, the money value is attached to money.

Think about it. When growing up, how much could you buy with a quarter? How much can you buy with $20 today? The value attached to a quarterback in the day is quite different from the value assigned to the same quarter today.

If we are not careful, we will end up in a rat race. Earn money, spend it all, earn some more and spend that as well. We may even throw in a few debts here and there which further tightens our spending belts. So we earn to pay debts, pay bills, enjoy a little luxury and do it all over again, and again.

However, deep down, what we want is to live a full life where we don't have to worry about money, how much we earn or spend. We want to be free to spend as much as we like but remain with enough surplus that we have more than enough to spend tomorrow on ourselves, our friends and family, and to share with the less fortunate.

Financial freedom is a journey. You must start by tracking your monthly expenses. How much do you spend on a bill? How about holidays and luxuries? Clothes and other home supplies? Transport and commute? Note down every instance you spend money and track it for some time. You will know exactly where your money goes.

It is easy to assume that we spend our money on essential things. Frankly, mostly we do, but some of these 'important' things are wants and not needs. Moreover, by indulging, we end up with little to nothing to save and invest.

Do you have money goals? Wishing you could spend money freely is a good goal, but it's a long-term goal. To achieve it, you need specific short-term goals that will steer you towards achieving financial freedom. How much do you want to save every month? Do you have a strategy on where you can draw more saving by tightening your expenditure? How about investment? What would be the best investment plan for your household?

The purpose of this book is to help you understand money, how it affects you (and those around you) and how you can keep it and invest it, so it earns you more.

Chapter 1: Where does your money go?

It's the end of the month, your salary just hit your account, and for the first time, you have called all your bills to a meeting. You have a calculator ready, a pen, your bills, and a sheet of paper with the total sum of your cash written in big letters.

One after the other, you write down everything you need to pay, and things don't look right. You need more than you can spare. You go through your list for the fifth time, trying to figure out what you can save, what can take a back seat, and what must be paid right away.

It's been hours, and you are still short. What do you? Should you take another loan? If you do, next month's expenses are going to be tighter, so that's not an option. You try to think of someone who can loan you some cash and come out blank. You owe almost everyone you know.

How did you end up here?

Diving into your expenses is scary, especially if they are in a mess. But don't let that discourage you. Every journey has a starting point, and for your expenses, the fixed starting point you need is knowing where your money goes.

Whether your starting point is worse than you realize, getting a real financial picture can help you figure out the next step to take. Every aspect of your finances matter. You can't focus on the big stuff and forget the small things. You need to look into every element that feeds your financial situation if your path to prosperity is to become clear.

Your financial picture has more than your bills, loans, and paychecks. Most of us focus on the familiar part, but to see the bigger picture, we must know what we need to look at. Here what you need to look at:

1. **Networth**

Your net worth refers to everything you owe of significance less your debts and liability. This could be your assets, investment, your home, any real estate, jewelry, and anything else of value. Liabilities include your car loan, mortgage, student's loan, and any other payables you need to make. Your net worth is your financial health. It clearly says what you would remain with if you sold all your assets and paid all your bills.

2. Cash flow

Personal cash flow looks at cash circulating in your account for a specified period. Cash inflow includes your salary, interests on savings accounts, dividends from your investments, capital gains from sold financial securities such as stocks and bonds. It also includes any income gained from selling assets such as houses and cars.

Cash outflow represents all expenses. This may include rent and mortgage payments, your monthly utility bills, groceries, entertainment, and gas. Any repairs on your car or house fall here.

3. Credit scores

A credit score refers to a number that measures your creditworthiness based on your credit history. Lenders such as banks will use this score to predict your probability of paying a debt.

4. **Your complete debt details.**

This will include your balances, the interest rates charged, your monthly contribution towards their payment, and the expected payoff dates.

5. **You must also look at your retirement account**. Look at your contribution, your balance, any asset allocation, and the average return.

Our expenses are usually what traps us in the financial race we so often find ourselves. Have you ever notices that as your income increases, so do your expenses? To harmonize your financial picture, start by tracking your daily expenses.

There are tons of apps you can download online that will help you track every dollar you spend. Be ready for surprises when you start this exercise. Your casual and credit spending is what skyrockets your monthly expenditure. You buy lunch every day, but when you look at the monthly expense, it will cost you about $200.

To track your expenditure and account for every dollar, you must follow every expense you made, but most importantly, you must track what you did with the balance. We are often tempted to ignore the quarters and loose change, but you would be surprised how much they account for at the end of the month.

At the end of the month, check your spending versus your income. How much did you spend against how much you earned? If your expense was less than your income, you could keep it as it is. If your spending was more than your income, buckle up for the ride.

Tracking your finances will help you empower your decisions. For instance, if spending $500 on entertainment every month makes you uneasy, you can easily cup that budget to $200. But you can't make that decision if you don't how much you spend on entertainment.

Rita is best friend with two ladies her age. They all work in different fields, and each makes a decent amount of cash. They have all bought houses and are comfortably paying their mortgage. However, Rita has been having trouble at her workplace and with her finances.

She pitched a project to her company and was tasked to head the operations and bring in the bucks. But things are not working out as she would have hoped. Her job is on the line, and she is petrified of what will have if she loses this job. Old habits die hard, so every weekend, Rita still goes out with her friends and spends around $150. Her finances are bleeding, but she would rather ignore the situation than face it.

A few days ago, she was called in by her boss. He was not pleased, and he gave her a few weeks to turn things around in her department, or he would have to find someone who could. For the first time since she started working, Rita called her bills, income, debts, and calculator for a meeting. Her girls called and asked if she would be joining them for an outing, and for once, she declined.

Instead, she downloaded her bank statement and wrote all her expenses down. From her analysis, she spends between $500 to $1,000 on wants a new bag here, a couple of pairs of shoes, new hair, and booze. Her savings are stagnated, and she was deep in debt. If she lost her job, she was fried!

How to eliminate unnecessary expenses
1. **Sharpen your financial awareness**

Rita is now aware of where her money is going. She has gone further to create a chart on how much she owes, whom she owes, and when they expect to be paid. If she is to survive this financial storm, she needs to make sharp decisions.

She has uncovered her spending leaks and budget overflows. Her first decision is to close all the holes that cause the leak.

2. **Note your fixed expenses**

Fixed expenses are the dollar amount that does not change. These include mortgage, student's loan, car loan, among others. From her list, Rita notes down all her fixed expenses. Her mortgage cannot go down, but where things stand, it is too high for one person. She lives alone in a three-bedroom house with a pool. The solution, get a roommate. It will cut her expenses by a third.

3. Cut your variable expenses

Variable cost refers to payments we cannot do without, but they vary from week to week, month to month. For instance, grocery shopping, water usage, power, and transport. One of Rita's best friends uses the same rout she uses to work. Rita vows to call her and ask if they could carpool. It will, after all, benefit both of them. She also noted the many food items in her fridge that are about to expire. She notes which ones she will stop buying and which ones she will buy in smaller quantities.

4. Cut your discretionary expenses

Discretionary expenses include anything that is based on your wants and needs. This includes things such as clothes, entertainment, memberships, among others. When cutting unnecessary costs, people usually have discretionary expenses in mind.

From Rita's analysis, she notes that she spends too much on entertainment, around $600. If she goes out once a month with her friends, she can cut this budget down to $150. But to keep her weekends interesting, she needs to find something to keep her engaged. She lists a few of her interests and how much they are likely to cost. Her total entertainment cost comes to $300.

Rita then calls all her favorite boutiques and cancels her subscriptions. She also cancels a few memberships to clubs she never goes to and caps her take out spending by half. In total, she will have an extra $1500 every month.

Cutting your expenses will involve many lifestyle changes, but spending modestly and avoiding overspending will help you achieve your financial success. The starting point has a clear current financial picture by tracking your expenses.

Chapter 2 Budgeting

Kevin is not at a good place, at least his finances are not. For as long as he can remember, he has been using a monthly budget to determine what he will do with his money, but someone, things are not working. Things are so bad that he is moving his family across town to live with his parents. He is at the lowest point of his life.

Why isn't his budget working? Where is he going wrong?

Whenever he sat down with his wife, they would usually calculate all their bills and allocate funds to each bill. They had specific financial goals they wanted to attain within a certain period, and when it was time to move, they would look for every means possible to reach the goal, commonly referred to as adjusting the budget.

When things fell apart, they were shocked and frustrated. Kevin and his wife thought they had everything in order, but clearly, they did not. They needed to go back to the drawing board.

What is a budget

A budget is known to make an adult's skin crawl. While we all know it is an essential tool to helping us manage our money, we tend to think of it as this tedious, bothersome task that is going to restrain us from doing the things we love.

The opposite is true, however, but before I explain, let us first define a budget. A budget is simply an estimation of your income and expenses for a given time. If your budget has been failing in the past, it could be because of either of these two reasons.

You budget lacks a clear financial picture of your past spending, or it requires clearly defined goals. Take a second and think about it. Your budget is nothing but a spending goal. Like Rita, you are telling yourself that you will not spend more than X amount on a given item. This is a goal. But for goals to be practical, they need to follow certain criteria.

They must:

1. Be specific. I will spend $150 on take-out and put $250 into savings or I will spend less than I earn this month.

2. It is measurable. As a rule of thumb, the budget will not work if you have no way of measuring what you earn and what you spend.

3. Attainable. I will keep my spending less than $1000 although my rent is $600 and my utility bills total $200. This cannot be attained. This is what was ailing Kevin and his wife.

4. Relevant. Most people get the first three parts right but fail from this step forward. To know if your budget is attainable, ask yourself why you are saving. Do you want to test your willpower, pay off your student's loan within a year, or meet a savings goal? Be clear with what you want.

5. It is time-bound. Your budget and financial goals need a deadline. For most people, it's the

end of the month, but a weekly budget goal is typically more effective.

Most budgets will be missing a few aspects on this list, whether they are not relevant, attainable, or measurable. Missing any of these aspects sets you up to fail.

Like most people, Kevin wanted to stop spending more than he earned, to pay existing debts, and to have extra money for a home, emergencies, retirement, and a vacation. There is only one problem with these goals. They are not specific enough. A more specific goal would be finding an extra $1000 to pay off your students' loan within a year and a half.

When you start budgeting, it is wise to start with one goal. A reasonable budget lets you see the whole picture in your spending, but biting more than you can chew is risky. Start with spending a little less on take-out, then add shopping next week.

If your goals are not specific, you will not be motivated to attain them. Broad goals are meant to help you determine what you want to achieve in the long run, but more specific goals help you achieve your broad goal.

Financial independence by retirement is a broad goal. Setting aside 10% of your income every month to invest will help you attain your broad goal.

Types of budgets

Budgets are not made equal, and your personality and goals should guide the budget method you use. People who are more disciplined with money tend to thrive when using a 50/30/20 budget. The budgeting categories remain flexible so you can adjust your spending every month depending on your needs. You must, however, stay within the broad categories to keep moving forward with your financial goals. 50% of your earnings go to your needs, 20% goes to savings and investments while 30% goes to your wants. This method allows you to have enough for your day-to-day operations while saving for your future and enjoying yourself.

The envelope system is excellent for people who have a problem with overspending. It is a cash-based method where you withdraw all the money you need to spend and split it into individual envelopes. Once an envelope is empty, you aren't lucky. You will have to wait for next month's budget or pull money from another envelope. Thanks to technology, you don't need tons of envelopes in your drawers. You can use apps that allow you to develop an envelope method and still use your debit and credit card.

If the envelop method and the 50/30/20 method have failed you, you might want to try the zero-based method. This method assigns every dollar for some work. If you earn $3000 a month, you must spend $3000 a month. You create budget categories and assign values to each group until your balance is zero. This method takes time to master, but once you do, you find that it expresses your values, which is a plus for many people.

Why is budgeting important
1. **You spend within your means**

Credit cards are an easy way to get something you want that you can't have, but often it's a means to spend on things you don't need. Budgeting helps you stay within your limits. Most people who misuse credit cards don't realize they are overspending until it's too late.

2. **Easy way to a happy retirement**

Spending your earnings wisely is essential, and saving for a happy future is critical. Budgeting helps you put money in your 401K. Investing your savings ensures you have a neat sum stashed away to for your future. Everyone would rather spend their retirement golfing and visiting exotic places, but this will remember a pipe dream if you don't budget today.

3. **You are prepared for emergencies**

Life comes with many surprises, some not so welcome. Ask yourself, how would your life be affected if you get laid off? What if you became sick and your insurance could not cover all the expenses? How would you be affected? Budgets often include emergency funds (separate from your savings) which are acts a cushion for when things go south.

How to stick to your budget

How come many people don't follow their budgets, even after spending so much time tracking their expenses and writing the budget? The answer is simple; they complicate it too much. A healthy budget should be enjoyable to follow. You should do important things but have enough left to do whatever you want.

A budget that creates a debt death spiral is one where you have your house paid, transport catered for, debt paid, and whatever remains is divided into everything else, usually without any cushion for the things you love.

An easy tip is to have a big-picture budget that leaves you with enough play money every month. Play money is not marked for anything in particular and may sometimes cover necessities like food, expenses that come every once in a while, like insurance premiums and car maintenance.

Another tip is simplifying your expense tracking. You can do this by automating your tracking. Automation makes sure you are on track most of the time. If you pay everything with a credit card, there are tons of budget tracking tools you can use, but if you don't fancy using an app, then you can result to traditional methods such as card statements. Have a pivot table with a general spend category.

Shortcuts such as the ones outlined here are a great way to keep you on track, but if you are not strict with yourself, you will end up leaving room for error. The idea is to make it as simple as possible but to follow it as strictly as possible. The more errors you have, the more likely it is, this will not work for you. You will continue with your old spending habits. The more transactions you track, the less likely you are to make errors.

Chapter 3: The easiest way to save

Getting started is usually the hardest thing when saving is a concern. "It's not how much money you make, but how much money you keep, how hard it works for you, and how many generations you keep it for."—Robert Kiyosaki. Saving when you have money is a simple fact often hard to learn. You could be overwhelmed, wondering how or where to start. In this chapter, we look at how you can save an extra buck in areas such as household expenses. We will help you develop an easy, realistic saving plan for your goals, either big or small.

Household expenses

We define home or household expenses as general living expenses. These include things like food, housing, and utilities. We divide the sum of these expenses among the household members. Whether it is between spouses or roommates. Other times these expenses are handled by a single person in the family, the breadwinner. Household expenses often include recurring purchases. To lessen the monthly expense load, many people look for ways to cut the costs.

So what qualifies as a household expense? We can divide household expenses into the following four areas:

Home expenses

Housing payments like rent, mortgages, real estate taxes, utility bills, house or property insurance. Every individual's needs in the family are also home expenses. This may include any healthcare and medication fees.

Child-related expenses

These mainly include any expenditures for education such as tutoring, buying and maintaining school uniforms, textbooks, PC's, stationery, paying for daycare or babysitter, and more. Since the child depends on the parent or guardian to pay these fees, they fall under household expenses.

Transportation expenses

You cannot cut out spending money on transportation because you have to get around. Whether it is going to work or school, most people cannot live without a car. From owning one to maintenance, cars can eat into your budget. Their value constantly decreases. Many extra costs come with having a car, from car payments, insurance, gas, parking, service, and repairs. So how can you reduce your automobile budget?

Entertainment expenses

Many look to cut back here when they consider ways to reduce their costs. You can spend a lot on leisure and pastime activities. As you budget for household necessities, the need for these expenditures come into question. Some of these expenses include nights out, going to the movies, television subscriptions, and vacations. Any money spent on hobbies like taking dance classes, collecting collectible items, membership fees to clubs or gyms should be included here.

How to save on home expenses
1. **Utilities**

Electricity and water rank high on the expense list. You can reduce your electricity bills by turning off the lights when they are not in use. Unplug any unused electronics such as the stereo or kitchen appliances instead of leaving them on standby. Air conditioners (AC) are among the most significant power consumers in the house. Regulating your thermostat can help avoid extreme temperature changes. Turn off the AC and use fans to circulate air in the house. Turn off pre-programmed utilities like the AC, heating or sprinkler systems. Use as much natural light as possible. Open windows and use mirrors to light up the house.

Switch from incandescent to more energy-efficient LED bulbs. Shorter showers and turned off the taps when brushing and shaving to conserve water. This reduces both your electricity and water bills. When purchasing electronics like refrigerators or washing machines, go for those certified as energy saving.

Internet, TV, and phone services are necessities of modern life. They can be bought separately or bundled at varying costs. Consider cutting back or bundling your phone, TV and internet services. Decide what you need in terms of data capacity and television channels. With cheaper TV alternatives like Netflix, Hulu or ShowMax you can do away with cable TV.

For items like toiletries and non-perishables, consider getting them in bulk. Watch out for discounts by window shopping a few places before you make a purchase. Look out for sales and bargains in different stores and see what you can get. Cut back on shopping in expensive stores and try thrift stores instead. If you use house cleaning services, consider trimming back and doing them yourself. Set aside time to handle these tasks, either daily or weekly. Get the whole family involved and delegate chores to keep things fun.

2. Food

When you go, grocery shopping always has a list. This keeps you focused and helps avoid impulse buying. Coupons, sales, and discounts can come in handy too. Don't shop while hungry, your stomach will overpower your brain, and you will end up overspending. The cost of food made at home is a lot cheaper than eating out. Try to make most of your meals at home. Carry packed lunches to work too. Start a garden and grow some herbs and vegetables such as greens. Many Do-It-Yourself sites can show you how to start a small garden. Find out what you can grow and what plants do well in your area.

3. Insurance

Consider moving to a less expensive house or area. Rural or suburban areas offer better housing options compared to living within the city. While insurance is essential, the premiums can get hefty. Insurance helps protect against the unexpected. Speak to someone at your office about the various options you have that can reduce your insurance costs. You can downgrade your health insurance. If you do not rely on regular medication or visit the doctor often consider a high deductible health insurance plan. A high deductible health plan is ideal since you only need coverage for a health emergency. Despite the saving made ensure you weigh the pros and cons of such a plan.

Most insurance companies have discounts ready if you bundle your home and car insurance policies together. Shop around and get quotes to help you get the best deal. Term life insurance is a cheaper alternative to life insurance. It matures when you retire and presumably don't have as many dependents. Life policies last for a lifetime, but the premiums are higher. Raising your deductibles can lessen your annual premiums, saving you some money.

4. Childcare

Cheaper childcare options are a great way to save, primarily if you work during the night and are home during the day. Compare various childcare options such as nanny sharing and pick the one with the best value. Look around on where to get affordable stationery and textbooks. Trading in books can help you get the ones you need at a lower price.

5. Transport

Use public transportation to get around. It is a great way to save more money on gas, maintenance, and parking fees. You can also forego having a car altogether. With the emergence of apps like Zipcar, Uber, and Lyft, you can live a car-free life. The ride-sharing feature in some of these apps, allow you to cost-share trips. This is a great way to save, especially for long trips.

If you choose to live a car-free life, consider selling your car. You can use the extra money to pay off debts or add it to your savings account.

Carpooling is another great way to save. You will save on gas and reduce the wear and tear on your car. Carpooling allows you to use designated carpool lanes, which can make getting to work easier. Apps like Zimride, RideScout, Uber, Hitch, and more have a lot of customizable features that can help you find a ride to wherever you are going. They allow for ride-scheduling either daily or weekly.

If you do not want to sell or stop using your car, there are ways you can make it more fuel-efficient. Hybrid vehicles are more energy-efficient than gas-only vehicles. Consider trading in your vehicle for a more fuel-efficient one. Ensure your tires are well inflated and in good condition. They can improve your gas mileage, getting you more value for the money spent on fuel. Regularly get your car serviced to ensure it is in good working condition.

Motorcycles and bicycles are other transport modes you can consider. Motorbikes use less fuel than cars and save you both time and money. Bicycles not only save you money but will also get your blood pumping. They are a great healthier option.

6. Subscriptions

To avoid debt or to have to forego things you need, consider canceling some of the memberships you have. Ask yourself, how often you use these services? If you are not a gym regular, pay only when you go to the gym. You can also work out at home with the tons of home workout videos available online.

Reduce or eliminate your cable bill by opting for basic cable instead of premium. Netflix, Hulu, and other streaming services allow you to see your favorite shows at a much lower cost. Some apps can allow you to view premium cable channels like ESPN. Search for inexpensive forms of entertainment. You can try going to local fairs or music festivals. Volunteering can also be a great way of spending your free time. Cancel any subscriptions you have for newspapers and magazines. Unless you like reading newspapers, you can read news online and stay informed.

Eliminate or reduce any consumable habits such as drinking and smoking. Other than being a constant drain on your budget, they pose health risks.

If the household expenses exceed your capacity to pay them, they will drag you into debt and frustrate your financial goals. T.T. Munger says, "The habit of saving is itself an education; it fosters every virtue, teaches self-denial, cultivates a sense of order, and broadens the mind." Trying out a few of these methods can result in huge savings down the line.

Trying all the money-saving tips could turn around your economic future. Decide which tips you will start with as biting everything at the same time will only frustrate you. Keep it simple an enjoyable. That's the secret to making a long-term change.

Chapter 4: How To Get Out Of Debt

In theory, staying debt free seems easy: don't spend more than you earn, and you will be debt-free. However, as most people can attest, being debt-free is more complicated than that. Our attitude toward money, its management, and spending can make getting into debt quite easy. For many of us, our financial mentality is to purchase now and pay later. With the widely available convenience of financing, family expectations, and misguided repayment times, one can get stuck in debt.

"Budget and you have more money to pay for necessities, entertainment, and to gratify your worthwhile desires without spending more than nine-tenths of your earnings." - George S.Clason

Before getting out of debt, you need to understand what it is. Debt is the sum of money you owe. There are many different types of debts. The most common bad debts are credit card debts, medical debts, and student loan debts. Personal loans, cell phone bills, utility bills, bank overdraft charges, car loans, payday loans are other forms of debts. Laws that govern debt collection mainly apply to consumer debt.

Good debt and Bad debt

There is a big debate on whether there is good debt. But without borrowing money, many people could not afford to buy a house, real estate investments, or a car. We define good debt as money borrowed and used to increase your net worth. Examples include education tuition such as college fees, starting a small business, investing in real estate. Good debt is taken to help one generate more income.

Bad debt refers to borrowing money to buy depreciating assets. Cars, new clothes, consumables such as vacations are examples of bad debt. Credit cards rank highest in bad debt. The interest rates on them are higher than on other consumer loans, and the repayment plans are designed to maximize costs for the consumer.

Placing good and bad debts is, however, not as easy as we may think. Depending on their financial situation, credit, and other factors, some debt can be good for some people but bad for others. Consolidation loans can benefit those with high-interest loans but are a terrible idea if you don't change your spending habits. They have lower interest rates, making them easier to pay off. Borrowing to invest carries its risks. The investment could fail, leaving you in deep debt. But you could profit and have extra cash. Before borrowing, check if you understand and are capable of covering the losses.

Anyone in debt wants to get out, or at least manage the debt. These tips will help you do exactly that and help you start the journey to managing your money better and find financial freedom.

1. **Reduce and eliminate your bad debt**

Train yourself to limit using one or two cards. Stop creating more debt. Ensure any new charges are fully paid every month to avoid long-term debt. This alone may not get you out of debt, but it is a step in the right direction.

2. **Increase your payment premiums**

Paying the minimum on your debts means it will take longer to clear your debts. While paying minimum payments, you will probably end up paying more than double what you were charged.

3. **Find ways to get extra income**

With proper financial education, understanding how money works and how to make it work for you can help you generate extra income. The additional cash can help with paying off debts, covering expenses, and increasing savings.

4. **Tackle one debt at a time**

Pay a debt at a time instead of spreading payments evenly on all of your debts. Meanwhile, make minimum payments to the rest of your debts. This plan can be applied to any debt. Start small by paying off outstanding credit cards and move on to car and mortgage payments. The more money you use to pay the debt, the faster you repay. Other than creating extra income, make a budget to manage your money better. It can also help you identify what to keep and where to cut back. Consider selling items you do not need to make extra cash.

5. **Ask for lower interest rates from your creditors**

Higher interest rates keep you in debt longer because most of the money pays off the interest charged. Very little goes to paying off the debt. If you have a good repayment history, you can easily negotiate for lower rates.

6. Borrow from your savings, retirement fund or life insurance policy

You can repay your debts with cash from your savings account or taking some money from your retirement fund. Channeling money from your retirement fund is only possible if you are close to retirement. If not, you will face early withdrawal charges and potential additional tax liabilities. The downside is you have less left over for retirement, and your interest also decreases. It is also an option to borrow from your insurance policy.

7. Settle your debt accounts with your creditors

Settling your debts include asking the creditor to take a one-time, lump-sum payment to cater for the debt. Creditors who accept a settlement offer also agree to cancel the rest of the debt. They only accept these offers from accounts that are in default or at risk of defaulting.

8. Pay off your debts through credit counseling

If your credit score disqualifies you from getting lower interest rates, try using a credit agency. They can help negotiate lower interest rates on your behalf and help ensure that you keep up with the payments.

9. Generate Wealth

Now that you are debt-free channel money towards investments. Build your asset column and generate enough passive income to cover your expenses. Keep reinvesting any extra cash into your assets to increase your revenue.

Increasing your financial intelligence can help you find more way to cut back and stay out of debt. *'The Richest Man in Babylon'* by George S. Clason is an excellent place to start. It has simple lessons on how to create and maintain wealth.

Clason says that to fatten your purse, set aside 10% of your earnings. You must also live within your means by spending less than you earn or earning more than you spend. Clearly define what a want is and what a need is. When your income increases, refrain from increasing your spending.

Once you have mastered the first and second step, make your gold multiply by making your money work for you. Learn about compound interest and its benefits. Investing is one thing, but guarding your investments is another. Insure your assets, create financial reserves, and avoid risky investments. Seek the advice of experts before investing.

A home is a great way to cut off debt since mortgage makes up the bulk of the debt people owe. Be smart about your most significant investment. Run the numbers and see whether owning a home is possible. Purchase a house that you can afford and enjoy it. Insure your future by having a retirement plan. Growing old is a reality for everyone. It is vital to plan for your retirement by looking for ways to maximize the earning potential of your retirement funds. Ensure your income is guaranteed even without you having a job. Keep your dependents in mind and remember that investment diversity can create safety for your money.

The seventh law dictates that you must increase your ability to earn by investing in personal development. Cultivating your financial IQ will make you wiser and more knowledgeable in money matters. With the internet, the information you need is closer to you that before.

In the five laws of gold, Clason indicates that we should have the following in mind.

1. Gold will come to you gladly if you increase the quantity to your keep, that is, one-tenth of his earnings. This way, you create an estate for your future and that of your family. As a bare minimum put away about 10% of your income.

2. Gold works diligently and contentedly for the wise owner who finds for it profitable

employment, multiplying even as the flocks of the field. If you invest well, your money will grow and work for you.

3. Protect your earnings by seeking the advice of experts. Invest only in what you fully understand. Talk to experts, read books, articles, and research thoroughly before you invest. We will talk more about this in a later chapter.

4. Gold slips away from the man who invests it in businesses or purposes with which he is not familiar or which are not approved by experts in the field. Take time to master the skills, attitude, and knowledge needed to handle investments and businesses.

5. Gold flees the man who would force it to impossible earnings. It escapes those who follows the alluring advice of tricksters and schemers, and who trust their inexperience and romantic desires in investment. Avoid get-rich schemes and scams. Always take caution when the deal is too good.

Finally, borrow sensibly, as the unintelligent use of debt will undoubtedly become a later burden. Read up on the most common types of debts, what to expect, and the ways to repay.

Chapter 5: Credit Cards

We live in an age of convenience. Banks are working harder to avail more money to their account holders. This has given rise to many products such as online banking, banking apps, debit, and credit cards. We know that they are small electronic plastic cards issued by a financial body. The difference between debit and credit cards is unclear to most people. They both offer convenience, remove the need to carry cash, and can be used in the same places. They even look alike.

The fundamental difference between the two is where each card pulls money from. A debit card takes it from your bank account. A credit card, on the other hand, lets a person borrow money at a point of sale (POS) to pay for goods or services. This is what has landed most of us in financial jail! Our credit scores have gone to the dogs, and we don't understand the changes that come with credit cards.

Credit cards are an easy way for you to buy. The Idea behind a credit card is simple. Borrow money and pay it back with interest. But, other charges accompany the card. For instance, there are charges levied for using a credit card during purchase. Let's say at the end of the month you get a bill of $1500 for using your card that month. The bank will send you this bill as an invoice of the purchases made within that month.

You have two repayment options. First, you could opt to pay the amount in full and before the due date. Paying in full means, you do not need to pay any interest or late fees. This is assuming you don't have any outstanding debts on the card. If you have a cashback rewards credit card, this repayment method can help you rack up much money in annual rewards over time.

The second option would be to pay the minimum payment due on the $1500 and pay back the rest over time. This is a fraction total owed for the billing cycle, which can either be 2% to 5% of the money. For the 1500 debt, the minimum payment you could make per month is somewhere between $30 and $75. This option carries with it interest penalties on the overdue amount and compounds it as long as you owe the debt.

How much you can borrow or your credit limit is determined by the card issuer based on the holder's credit rating and credit history. You may hear terms like 'maxed out', which means that the cardholder has borrowed the maximum amount of money allowed for that card.

Certain factors determine the interest rates on a credit card. One's credit rating and history can influence the interest rate charged on their card. It can range between 10% to 25% or even higher. The card issuers can raise the interest rate if the credit rating of the borrower drops. The interest also raises when the national lending rates increase. There are no laws that dictate or cap interest rates for credit card issuers. This leaves the cardholder vulnerable to paying higher interest and more money than they borrowed.

Here are some credit card terms you should know
Zero balance

When a credit cardholder pays off any outstanding balance, their bill will read zero balance. A card user can have a zero balance by paying off the amount due in full or by not using the credit card. Paid off balances keep the cardholder's overall debt low. Lenders like credit card users who do not use up all their available credit because they can raise the credit rating to maximize their profits.

Annual fees

This is a yearly fee charged by credit card issuers to cardholders for using their credit cards. This fee is added to the customer's invoice statement. Not all cards have annual fees. Reward and travel credit cards, cards for those with bad credit, or those with luxury perks are prime examples. You can pick cards that have no annual fees charged.

Pros and cons of using a credit card

Credit cards protect your money. They protect you from losses due to fraud. If you lose your debit card to a thief, the money they use is withdrawn from your account instantly. It can cause late or missed payments on legitimate expenses. Overdue or defaulted payments can lower your credit score.

It also takes a while for fraudulent transactions to be investigated and reversed. With credit cards, if you suspect any fraud notify the issuer and don't pay for any purchases you did not make. The credit card company then investigates and resolves the matter.

You get signup bonuses as a welcome aboard benefit. Good credit rating can qualify you for higher rewards.

Continuous use of credit cards earns you rewards and points which can be redeemed. Get a card whose reward system matched your spending patterns.

Cashback credit cards refund a certain percentage of your balance despite what you have bought or where you bought it. This percentage ranges from 2% to 6 %.

With an affiliated credit card, a user can earn frequent flier miles. Cardholders accumulate miles at a rate determined by the airline. With the large mileage sign up bonuses, one can cash in and get a free flight within a short time.

Paying with credit cards is a great way to keep vendors honest. Let's say you get some work done in your house. But after you have paid the contractor the said work such as tiling, starts shifting or coming apart. If you paid cash or with a debit card, it is hard to get justice. With a credit card, the issuer can withhold the funds in dispute, allowing for repairs to be made. If repairs cannot be done, the bank can help you get a refund.

Paying for purchases with a credit card offers you a grace period. Debit card purchases are instantaneous. With credit cards, the money stays in your checking account until you clear your card bill.

Many credit cards come with many consumer protections that many people are not aware of. These include travel insurance and product warranties that surpass the manufacturer's warranty.

Credit cards are universally accepted. Some purchases like renting a car or hotel room are easier with a credit card than a debit card. Credit cards allow the hotel or rental car company to charge you for any damaged.

Using a credit card responsibly can help build your credit rating. The credit card company is obliged to report your repayment history is reported to credit bureaus. A good history can help improve your score. The inverse is also true.

Using a credit card may not be right for you if:

You cannot pay your balance in full and on time. If you find this happening more than once, stick to cash or debit card purchases.

You easily overspend. Spending more than you can afford, it will lead to debt. If you are not careful, you may end up buried under debt. Paying off this debt will reduce the money your active income.

Surpassing your credit limit leads to costly fees and can lower your credit rating.

There are times when paying cash or with a debit card is better than using a credit card. Retailers give bigger discounts on cash sales, although you forego the protections that come with credit cards.

Safeguarding your Credit

When it comes to identity theft, both a credit card and debit card have equal risks. Contact your bank immediately if you think your credit or debit card data has been compromised. Take further precautions and track your credit report to ensure your identity has not been stolen. It is necessary to check your statements monthly to guarantee that you can identify all charges made. You can easily identify any fraudulent fees and get them reimbursed. Banks limit the period when you can report a fraudulent charge on your card. So, promptly notify them of anything suspicious.

It is important to note that credit cards can lead to debt racking up quite easily. There are many ways to control credit card debt. Tackle the biggest debt first. Once you are done, move to the next one until all your balances are cleared. You may be tempted to cancel your cards to curb debt, but this can hurt your credit rating.

Before canceling your card, ask yourself if you need to. If you find yourself spending too much or you are paying annual fees for a card, then cancelation is called for. Canceling a credit card involves more than just cutting it up. Follow these steps to cancel a credit card properly.

Find the right person to contact and let them know that you wish to cancel your card.

Redeem any rewards or points on the card. If you can transfer them to another card, do so.

Clear all balances on the card by either paying it in full or moving it to another card with favorable terms. Confirm with the credit card issuer that the card has no outstanding balances.

Write a letter to the bank requesting to close the card account and follow up to ensure it is marked closed.

Keep notes throughout the process in case anything goes wrong or for reference. Once all this is done, you can dispose of your card however you wish. Many people prefer cutting it up.

Credit cards are best used by those who are disciplined and can pay off their balances on time and in full. Credit cards call for responsibility. They can be an excellent asset when you need to make a purchase, and you want to avoid using cash or your debit card. With the many rewards, protections, and the value of cash-in-hand, credit cards are not all bad.

Chapter 6: Start Saving

So far, we have covered the importance of a budget and why you should follow one, how to get rid of debt and where you can make savings on your daily expenses. So far, you are doing great. You made it to this section, so kudos for being committed to the journey.

When your finances are messy, it's hard to imagine that you will have anything left to save. After all, you are technically in deep debt, and just because we have talked about great out-of-debt tips does not mean your financial situation has changed. At least not yet. So how will you manage to set aside some money for investment and a rainy day?

Speaking of rainy days, have you ever noticed how it rains immediately you start setting money aside for it? Also, why is it that your salary is on the rise, but your bank account is not? You are not alone.

Penny is a stockbroker. For years she has been working as a waitress and doubling up as a bartender on the weekends to make ends meet. But now, things are in a good place. Her income has surged from $5000 a year to over $50,000 a year, but there is only one problem.

She is in more debt than she was when her income was lower. She can barely make her bills, and she has missed her credit card payments for a few times. What's the logical thing to do? Earn more money! So, she goes ahead and works harder, managing to double her current income.

Just like that, she goes from eating French fries for lunch to eating lunch at a fancy hotel, her wardrobe gets spruced up, and she finally ditches her old vehicle for a new car, which she finances. But still, her bank account looks as empty as it was when she was earning $5000 a year. She is more broke than ever.

Penny is not alone. Most people try to make up for lost when they get new cash flow. They can finally eat out as often as they want, go for nicer vacations, and fill their lives with whatever they want. Who wouldn't want a little playtime with $100,000 a year? When you go out with your friends (who earn less than you), you feel obliged to pick up the tab.

Success is not solely about making money. According to financial advisers, there are three parts to money, and for you to be genuinely financially free, you need to master all of them.

1. **How to earn money**

The thumb rule of earning money is simple; the value you offer others is equivalent to how much money you earn. If you earn $5000 a year, that's how much value you are offering.

2. **How to keep money**

When you earn money, how much of it do you keep for yourself? We are going to discuss this in a short bit because that's where savings come in.

3. **How to invest money**

How much of the money did you keep works for you? We will discuss more of this in the next chapter.

How to keep money

For Penny to get out of her murky financial situation, she needs to pay her debt and put some money aside to cushion herself in case of emergencies. Her credit cards have hit six figures, and the interest rate is at least 21%. Despite things looking bleak for her, Penny must start saving immediately! Debt or not!

Wait. What? However, I have no money to spare?

That's precisely why you need to spare some. One of the keys to getting out of your situation is to start immediately! Think about it, you have no fall back plan, and in the harsh economic times we live in, anything could go wrong. The time to start building your reserve is now.

In chapter 4, one of the tips we gave from the book "*The Richest Man in Babylon*" is to set aside 10% of your income. This is your reserve. Let's assume you have $100. Your finances are everywhere, and you could use every cent you have, and even more.

However,...

If you spend the full $100, will you have enough? Probably not. If you save $10, will you have enough? Again, not likely.

It won't matter if you spend the full $100 or not. You will need more than $100 to get out of your situation. But saving $10 out of the $100 starts fattening your purse. What happens when you save $10 for ten months? You have an extra $100.

It's a hard pill to swallow, especially when things don't seem like they are working out. As we have already stated, you can get this extra money from reducing your expenses, be they fixed, variable, or discretionary costs.

Once you have comfortably started saving 10% of your income, increase the amount you save whenever you minimize debt or finish paying it altogether. Saving is not meant to strain you or cause you heartaches. It's meant to excite you. The only risk is not saving if you view your savings as meager. Don't look at it from 'now' perspective but as a long-time goal.

How to start saving

Famous finance expert like Suze Orman and Dave Ramsey have the same advice on where to begin saving.

1. **Load your emergency fund**

You need enough money to cater for eight months of living expenses. Within eight months, you are likely to have found a solution to your lack of income, whether it's getting a new job, starting a business, or expanding your income.

2. **Save daily**

A habit is formed when the motivation is strong, and when it is repeated. Actively saving money towards your goal will cultivate the habit of saving, even when you save a dollar a day. Start by changing your perspective about saving. If you view it as a bother, start by seeing it as something that will benefit you. This will motivate you to change. The small steps you make will change your brain and neural mechanisms associated with saving in your memory. The more you take the steps towards saving, the stronger these connections become, and the easier saving becomes. This may seem like automating savings, but the more you become comfortable with it, the easier it gets.

3. **Make it visible**

To develop the habit of saving and stick to it, you need to see your money accumulate. Use a savings jar or an online account where you can see your savings increase substantially as you load your account. Having visible signs will provide you with feedback and act as a form of encouragement. The more the account grows, the more you are proud of yourself, which results in wanting to maintain the growth.

4. **Spend less than you earn**

We have discussed this in the previous chapters so that we won't dwell on it so much. However, I feel it is important to emphasize its importance to saving and your financial journey. Forming a saving mindset means you abandon a spending mindset. When your purse begins to fatten, you will be tempted to spend the money on something you have been eyeing for a while, or something you think you might need. Before you remove your credit card, ask yourself this quest: I want this item, but do I need it? If I don't buy this item today, will my life continue to function normally? If your answer is yes, you are dealing with a want. Walk away. The more you do it, the easier it becomes.

There is the peace of mind associated with having a savings account. Research has shown that people who save have more peace where money is a concern than people who don't save. Besides knowing that you have a fall back plan, you are also more comfortable making rational money decisions.

Chapter 7: Increasing Your Income

So far, we have managed to budget our money, get out of debt, and build an emergency fund. These are some of the ways you can increase the cash in your bank.

Let's assume you have everything right. Your budget is working, your emergency fund is healthy, and your debts are under control. Do you stop there? Far from it. Once you have a healthy financial working system, it's time to increase your income.

For some people, this means managing your career effectively by finding the right job, knowing when to ask for a raise, and knowing the right time to move on. For others, it means selling things they already own, perusing a money-making hobby, or starting a business. Now, we are going to look at all these ways and explain how you can utilize them to increase your income.

How to increase your income at work

Your health is a valuable asset, but your career comes in at a close second. The ultimate goal of every human being is to be happy. When you are sick, it takes away your joy, and when you are broke or when your career stagnates, it takes away your happiness.

It is possible to have a positive income without cash flow, and for most people, the cashflow comes from their jobs. You must make the best out of your income. But how do you choose a career path? Should you choose a career you love and follow the path regardless of how much you earn, or should you choose a job based on how much money you will make?

There is no correct answer to these questions. Finding a fulfilling career that will sustain you financially is not a walk in the park. You may end up not enjoying your job if you can't pay your bills and live a comfortable life. With a little persistence, you will live a fulfilled life if you choose to follow your passions. According to Paul Graham an author and venture capitalist, you may find work in your chosen path, but even then, you will not be free to work on what you truly love until you are in your thirties and forties. If you know the work you like, you are practically there.

You must have heard people say that if you do what you love money will follow you or the famous saying that a job is just a job, you are not meant to like it. There are many people who enjoy fulfilling careers and make a tidy sum while at it. Even then, these dream jobs didn't appear magically. To truly be happy at work, start by having a goal in mind. Don't pick a job because it pays well. Choose a field in your interest and experience, and have a goal of where you want to go.

According to Napoleon Hill, there is a simple formula you can use to choose a fulfilling career. First, make a list of occupations that interest you. Next, to the jobs, write a list of people who have succeeded in the profession. You must have access to these people or a way to access them. Book an appointment with them and make a list of questions you will ask them. Cover every aspect. If you are starting, ask them about their journey, how it was getting starting, and the challenges they have faced to get where they are.

Jim Collins, in this book "*Good to Greatness,*" came with another formula. He states that there is a sweet spot between passion, excellence, and economics. Think about what you are passionate about, what you do best, and what people are willing to pay you to do. Then you will find your sweet spot. The sweet spot is where the work you love, what you are good at, and what can earn you a living reside.

Is it possible to be good at something, have people willing to pay you for it, and still hate your job? Absolutely! Unfortunately, many people end up in this situation. If this is you, go back to the drawing board, get your sweet spot, and make the change.

How to negotiate your income

The money you make is directly equivalent to the service you render, but if you are not good at negotiating salary, your buddy who does the same job you do may earn twice as much as you do. If you want to see an increase in your bank account, learn how to negotiate for higher pay. The time to negotiate your salary is during performance reviews and when you are offered a job. Negotiation makes many people uncomfortable, but they are incredibly vital.

According to Jack Chapman in this book *"Negotiating You Salary"*, most of us accept what we are offered and spend little to no time negotiating for higher pay. We spend zero minutes negotiating. Negotiating for what you are worth can make a difference of thousands of dollars over your lifetime.

However, a salary increment does not start at the negotiation table. It begins at making yourself a desirable employee. You must offer much value if you are to position yourself to get a better salary. Businesses know that a valuable employee is worth keeping, and if it costs them a little more, they are willing to make the change.

When asking for a raise, be sure to have evidence of what warrants the increase. Ensure that you have met your deadlines, your employer is meeting their goals, and your efforts are directly affecting the positive growth of your company. Have a figure in mind and approach your employer about it. During the meeting, remain positive and make your case without complaining. Focus on your strengths and what you have accomplished during the time you have been with the company. Forget about the workload and other employees. You are not here to talk about their workload or their salaries. Focus on yourself.

Chapman says that the best time to ask for a raise is after a massive win on a project, after a strong performance review, and after your boss accords you new responsibilities. Keep in mind that a raise is not an entitlement. Just because you come to work every day does not make you entitled to a raise. Doing a good job gives you the right to ask for one.

What if your boss denies it? Ask them when you can revisit the topic. The economy has hit your company hard as it has every individual. Ask your boss what would warrant you a raise and work your best to achieve the set goal.

What else can you do?

Sometimes, a raise and a promotion are not always an option. With the economy down the toilet, it is harder to get a raise today than it was a few decades back. So, what can you do to increase your income?

- Use your company's retirement plan. Most companies will match your contribution. Don't turn down free money; take it.

- Improve your skills. You may not qualify for a raise this year, but you can increase your odds for future considerations if you improve your skills. Go for seminars, attend training sessions, and get certified in job-related fields.

- Ask for a different reward. Sometimes companies may not have enough money for a raise, but they may be willing to give you an extra week for vacation, a flexible schedule, so you have more free time, and better parking.

- Read the policies. An employee handbook is not exactly exciting to read, but you may find some perks you were not aware you could ask for.

- Build networks. Whether they are at your workplace or outside your workplace, build your network. Taking on tasks will strengthen your resume, and put you in the spotlight where your employer will notice you. Networks are also a great way to better opportunities with higher pay.

Multiple sources of income

Having a job is great, but it is important to diversify your sources of revenue. The risk of depending on one stream of income is if the stream dried up, you are fried. There are many things that could go wrong. Even fortune 500 companies go under, and you find yourself out work. To paint a better picture, here are a few reasons why you should never depend on one income source.

1. **To protect yourself from market fluctuations**

Market fluctuations can occur in your industry or across the country. Either way, your source of income may be affected. In 2008, the global economy was hard hit, and thousands of people lost their jobs unexpectedly. If this were to happen again, you would have another source of income to back you up.

2. **The easiest way to becoming wealthy**

Multiple sources of income are the easiest way to become wealthy. Each source will increase the amount of money in your bank account, presenting another path to advancement. It makes it easy for you to hit your financial goal. If one side is not steady, you can compensate with income from another stream.

3. **Offers more flexibility for the future**

Your future has more flexibility once your sources of revenue become steady. If you decide that you no longer enjoy your job, you will have an option of leaving without worrying where your next paycheck will come from, safety net or not. You also have the flexibility to seize investment opportunities when you have liquid cash; you can easily access.

How to have a second source of income

1. **Have a plan**

A budget is vital for your finances, and a business plan is critical for entrepreneurial success. For a small business, your plan may be a list of goals you want to achieve. If you need outside funding, you need a plan that's as detailed as possible.

2. Don't quit your day job

The world of business is pretty volatile, so quitting your day job is not in your best interest when you are starting. Start working at your business during the weekends and evenings. You can use this time to gauge if you want to do this full time or not.

3. **Find a mentor**

Having a guide is always helpful when you are walking into unfamiliar territory. Find a good lawyer who can give you advice on the legal implications of your business, and heed the advice your mentor gives you. If you are not an accountant, have one who can give you an accurate financial picture of your business.

4. **Keep your business and personal accounts far from each other**

Have an account specifically for your business and document everything that enters and leave that account. The risk of mixing the two is knowing where to draw the line. If one account is suffering, you take ages to notice because funds from the other account will blind you.

5. **Have an exit strategy**

You need to know your goals, why and how to get there. Are you building a business so you can sell it? Alternatively, is it something you will do for a few years and drop it? If things go south, how will your finances be affected, and how will you cushion yourself from falling into a pit?

In the world we live in, there is no shortage of the extra income streams you can create. From residual income to passive income, you can be sure you will find something that will fit your bill. Below are a few ideas of where you can start.

1. **Get a second job**

Is your schedule at your regular job more flexible? Consider getting a second job in your spare time. You can also maximize on the evenings and weekends to earn money. A second job does not necessarily mean getting hired by a different company. If you are skilled in a particular area, you can look for freelance opportunities where you offer your services to others for a fee. Do you love DIY projects? Look for items you can refurbish and sell them for a profit.

2. **Start a home business**

You may not be interested in owning a company that you work at full time, but a small-scale venture may be a good option for you. Can you start a business around a hobby you enjoy? You may not get rich when you play the piano at a wedding, but it will give you some extra cash for something you already know how to do. Are you good at baking? Sell some cupcakes or cookies to earn extra money and scale your home business when you have enough cash flow.

3. **Royalty income**

Royalty income refers to the payment you receive when others use your intellectual property such as copyright, patents, and trademarks. When you allow others to use your property, they pay you a fee for permitting them. You can do this with your music, stock photography, patent products, books, and minerals mined from your property.

4. **Rent out a small property**

Real estate is proven as one of the best ways to increase your income. If you have a property in the woods that you don't use as often, rent it out and earn a monthly income from it. Do you have a vacation home? This is another excellent source of income during the high and low season. An apartment in the city? Put it up on a site such as Airb&b and earn a tidy sum when someone rents it.

5. **Start an online business**

There are tons of business you can do online. You can start an e-commerce store or start dropshipping where you sell other people's products for a commission. You can start an affiliate marketing site, sell books on amazon/kindle, or become an influencer. Ultimately, you can create your products where you sell courses, apps, or mentor people for a fee.

To earn more, you need to put in the extra effort. There are no short cuts, but like Tony Robbins says, "success leaves clues." Follow the steps the people who have gone before you have used, and stop trying to reinvent the wheel. Stop overthinking things and remain flexible to try different formulas until you find one that is working for you.

Whichever income-generating activity you choose will need you to have skills, blogging is a skill. Selling is a skill. Crafting is a skill. The more you work at becoming better, the better you become. One essential skill you need to harness is marketing. If you have good products that people don't know about, they won't earn you money. Marketing is critical to the success of your business.

Every aspect of personal finance will not lack some naysayers. Some people think that building wealth means you are greedy and selfish. Some believe that you can't earn more than a certain amount, while others believe that money is evil. Don't be surprised when others say you are trying to overcompensate for something or lacking something. The most important thing is how you think and feel about it.

If like most people you think you can't earn more, you are right. If you believe you don't deserve more money, you will self-sabotage yourself until you can't earn past a certain amount. You must change the wiring of your brain first, and accept the benefits that come with earn more of this medium of exchange. Going by the words of Henry Ford, "whether you believe you can or can't, you are probably right." Change your mindset and thought patterns surrounding money, do the work, and stick to the plan until you increase your income.

Chapter 8: Investing Your Money

In chapter3, we mentioned the three main aspects of money. How to earn money, how to keep it, and how to invest it. So far, we have covered how to make money in chapter seven, where we looked at the different ways you can increase your wealth. In chapter three, we dived into how to keep money by looking at saving your money and maintaining a safety net.

In this chapter, we look at what will finally bring you the financial freedom you desire. That is, how to invest money. Investing is the ultimate form of passive income and the accelerator of financial independence. When you invest your money, you make money on your money, so you don't have to exchange your time for money.

Many people find investing confusing, even daunting, so they shy away from making any investment or make the wrong investments. Some invest too little or get ripped off by financial managers. Don't get distracted by complicated strategies or by the many gurus who promise you high returns within a short period.

What you need to focus on is gaining investment skills and growing your money as quickly as possible and as efficiently as possible. The longer you wait, the more time and money you waste. You don't need to figure everything out before you start. Every day you lose is a day lost that could have earned you money.

This does not mean you gamble your money away. That's not investing. When you invest your money, you send it out to work for you. You put it into something that gives you a chance to earn back your money and a profit on top of it. Gambling is relying solely on luck. When you invest, you should control some, if not most, of the variables that impact making back your money or variable that can affect your loss of capital.

You must minimize your risk, fees, taxes on contributions, taxes on withdrawals, but maximize your returns at the same time. All investments carry some form of risk, and it is juvenile to think that you can control the market, the economy, or the performance of your stock. However, by investing in the level of risk you are most comfortable in, you can get the highest level of return and maximize your chances for success. Your sweet spot is investing in a way that earns you as much money as possible but still allows you to get a good night sleep.

Warning: Approach with caution

- Always invest in what you understand. Don't put money in an investment you don't understand. You must understand the risk you are taking and the expected rewards.

- Beware of shiny investment. Anything promising 20% return within a few weeks or every year is a shiny invaluable object. It is unlikely to happen.

- Focus on simple financial instruments with consistent returns over time. It does not matter how much someone else recommends an investment.

- Spread your portfolio to include stocks, bonds, real estate, and other investments

- Only hire a financial advisor if they will teach you the ropes. Once you learn, invest your own money. Your chances of earning more are higher when you invest by yourself.

Start investing small amounts of money

What is your risk appetite? This is a question everyone looking to invest cash needs to answer. Your risk appetite is the tolerance you have with how your money will fluctuate with the market change. You are either a low-risk investor, moderate risk investor, or a high-risk investor.

• Low-risk tolerance is investors who are more conservative with their options. They prefer little to no fluctuation in investment and earning. They prefer to secure the initial capital. The interests earned in these investments are low.

• Moderate risk tolerance is investors who prefer more economical investment options. They are not entirely shy of risk but prefer a more balanced approach. They will invest in equal combinations to provide current income with moderate interest earned.

• High-risk tolerance investors, on the other hand, prefer more aggressive investment options. The potential for higher returns outweighs the risk of losing money, but the risk of losing their initial investment is high.

With this in mind, let us consider how to start investing your money.

Step 1: separate your short-term and long-term goals

You should invest your money depending on how soon you need the money back. Do you want to see the return in the short-term (less than five years) or the long-term (more than five years)?

Short-term investments

Short-term investments usually work best in low or moderate risk tolerance. This is mainly because your initial capital will be secured, and you will still earn interest on the money you invest.

If your goal is to have your dream vacation, the stock market would not be the best place to invest your money. The market could change tremendously within the five years, which may negatively affect your payment.

You might want to hold your short-term investment in cash in a savings account where you can easily access your money in case of an emergency. Remember the emergency fund you were building; this is where you should invest it.

However, always keep at least two months home expenses in cash, and have the rest working for you in the market. You can invest this surplus in low-risk investments that allow you to access your money within a week or two.

Keep your investment in bonds issued by a company or government. A bond is a loan with a guaranteed interest attached. Bonds are bought for some time, so be sure not to need this money anytime soon.

Long-term investment

This type of investment is best for people who plan to retire in style and live off their investment for the rest of their lives. You must take advantage of the power of compounding. If you want to retire for thirty years, for example, leave the investment and compound it for thirty years. Do not withdraw the interest. Instead, the interest should be part of the principal investment in the next year.

Whether you are investing for the long haul or for a short time, diversify your investment and refrain from having all your eggs in one basket. If one venture fails, the others will cushion you. Have bonds, real estate, stocks, and other forms of investment in your portfolio.

Step two: how much money do you want to invest

The more you invest, the more you earn. But when it comes to investing, you can start anywhere. The idea is to begin. Once your portfolio starts to fatten, and you stabilize your financial situation, you can always increase the amount of money you invest. Have in mind how much you want to invest every day, every month, and every year, then stick to the plan.

The best way to increase your investment portfolio is to increase your investment by a certain amount after every thirty days. For instance, if you plan to set money aside every week, commit to increasing your weekly investment by 1%. This will motivate you to increase your income through the means discussed in chapter 7. It will also help you tighten your spending belt.

You must be tempted to think that investment is a sacrifice, but let's change your mind a bit. Investment is the peace of mind. Sacrifice is a chore, and when you think about investment that way, you may not follow through with your plans. Instead, think of it as creating a safety net, a more relaxed future, and getting peace of mind.

Step 3: allocate your assets a target

How much money to do you want to keep in your low, moderate, and high-risk investments? Your objective should be determined by the level of risk and reward of your investment as well as the time you plan to invest.

This is a vital decision in investment. Generally, stocks are at high risk, so the more you invest in shares, the riskier your investment is due to market change. Bonds are less risky, but the returns are also significantly lower than stocks. Cash is cash. It will not earn you any interest over time. It will depreciate due to inflation.

Step 4: evaluate the fees and keep them as low as possible

Investment fees have an impact on how fast your money grows, how much money you will have in a given time, and how long it will take you to be financially independent. The higher the fees you pay, the less money you make. A 1% fee may not seem like much, but it adds up over time and affects your payment. If you are younger, the fees have more impact because they will compound more over the years. A small difference in fees will potentially subtract thousands of dollars from your earnings

Every dollar you invest makes a difference. You may start small, but through compounding, your investment will grow to $10,000 faster, then $100,000, and so on. Don't be afraid of mistakes, especially if you are younger. As you make mistakes, you learn.

Real estate investment for beginners

Learning to invest in real estate may be an uphill task, but once you are familiar with the market terminologies, things become more manageable.

You will be bombarded with many options, but before you start investing, think of how investing in real estate helps you achieve your financial goals.

As a real estate investor, you will make money in several ways. You can either buy and flip homes, invest in rental properties, or invest in commercial real estate. These methods will require you to handle the property yourself and to make several considerations. For instance, you must consider your flipping timeline, the location of your rentals, and the tax implication on your rentals.

Buying real estate investment trust or REITs, however, allows you to invest in real estate without owning any property. REITs pay high dividends, which make them an excellent investment. If your purpose is to save for retirement and not regular income, REITs will work perfectly for you.

An excellent beginner investment idea in the real estate business is renting out a room. You don't take on long-term tenants, and Airbnb will always prescreen your tenants. You are also protected against any damage your host may cause, which is a plus for you.

Investing in stocks for beginners

There are several ways to handle investing in stocks. For starters, you can choose to use an online broker. These brokers primarily deal with higher-net-worth clients and charge a substantial fee. Robo-advisors use technology to lower costs for investors and streamline the investment advice they offer you.

Your employer could also be a great way to get into stocks investment. If you are on a tight budget, invest one percent of your salary into your retirement plan. This money is usually invested in mutual funds, and sometimes in your company's stock.

When opening a stocks account, check the minimum balance you are required to deposit, or your account will not be accepted. You will find firms that will allow you to open an account with as little as $1000, but it pays to shop around before you decide which broker is best for you.

Check the broker fee and see if you will be paying per trade. Some brokers will charge you a commission of $2 per trade while some will charge as high as $10. Some will charge you no fees at all, but they will make up for it in other ways. Like mentioned earlier, the fees can quickly add up and affect your profitability.

Besides the mutual fees, you need to purchase a mutual fund which comes with its pack of fees. Also, check if the broker you are working with charges a sales load fee before buying the fund. Check their list of no-load funds, as well as a no-transaction-fee fund to avoid paying these extra charges.

Conclusion

Everyone has an opportunity to grow their money and get out of debt, but you must start to make this a reality. Be warned, though, when your income starts to grow, it is easy to fall into temptation and start spending more than you are earning again.

Refrain and continue saving and investing your money. Every small step counts. Every coin kept and invested counts. If you use the profit you make, you will be unable to grow your wealth. Instead, allow your investment to grow by using the profits as part of the next years principal. With time, you will have a venture that can not only buy you whatever you want but one that will continue to grow over the years.

Taking advice from experts in the field you wish to invest is critical to your investment. Would you go to a farmer when you are sick, or would you seek out a doctor? The same way, take your investment knowledge from those who understand the market dynamics and can offer you advice to help grow your investment.

Manage your credit cards with responsibility, or they will sink you into a hole. The easiest way to get into debt is to spend more than you earn. You need to keep your expenses lower than your income at all times. Watch your credit card spending because that's how we often find ourselves overspending.

To get out of debt is to pay. The longer it takes you to pay, the higher the interest rate you will be required to pay. Either consolidate your debt or tackle one debt at a time. You might want to reduce your expenses, so you have more money to spread around. Always start by saving 10% of your income. A safety net is essential for your peace of mind.

Budgeting does not have to be complicated. The more you simplify it, the better. As long as you track your expenses and stick to your budget, it will work for you. Ensure that you don't view it as a task but as a necessary tool to help you stay ahead, get a real financial picture, and manage your money correctly.

Each chapter in this book holds nuggets that will be valuable to you and those around you. Read this book and re-read it. Practice the tips outlined and stay focused and disciplined. Write your financial goal and stick it where you can see it every day,

and it will motivate you to keep working on your plan and to achieve your goal.

Reading List

Clason, George. *The Richest Man in Babylon*. United Kingdom: Penguin Random House, 1926.

Collins, Jim. *Good to Greatness.* United Kingdom: Willian Collins, 2001.

Chapman, Jack. *How to Negotiate Your Salary*. California: Ten Speed Press1987.

Hill, Napoleon. *Keys to Success.* United Kingdom: Penguin Publishing Group, 1994

Bryan, Elizabeth. *How to Get Out of Debt, Burn Your Mortgage, and Live a Life of Total Financial Freedom*. New Yolk: Wealth Liberty Institute, 2004.

Robbins, Tony. *Money Master the Game: 7 Simple Steps to Finical Freedom*. New Yolk: Simon & Schuster, 20414.

Printed in Great Britain
by Amazon